FINDING
PEACE

*Letting Go
And Liking It*

Paula Peisner Coxe

Sourcebooks
Inc.
Naperville, Illinois

Published by: **Sourcebooks, Inc.**
P.O. Box 372
Naperville, Illinois 60566
(708) 961–3900; FAX: (708) 961–2168

Design: Wayne Johnson

Library of Congress Cataloging-in-Publication Data

Peisner Coxe, Paula, date.
  Finding peace: letting go and liking it /
Paula Peisner Coxe.
        p.   cm.
      ISBN: 1-57071-014-7
      1. Peace of mind.   I. Title.
BF637.P3P46   1994
170'.44– – dc20   94–18067
                                              CIP

Printed and bound in the United States of America
10 9 8 7 6 5

TABLE OF
CONTENTS

INTRODUCTION 1

THE YOU OF
YESTERDAY 11

CHILDHOOD 15

PARENTS 21

MISTAKES 27

FORGIVENESS 31

ACCEPTANCE 35

PURPOSE 39

TABLE OF CONTENTS

UNDERSTANDING.................43

PRIDE.................47

EMOTIONS.................51

OBSTACLES.................55

BAGGAGE.................59

THE YOU OF TODAY.......63

PERMISSION.................65

ATTITUDE.................71

SILENCE.................77

TOLERANCE.................81

THE PRESENT.................87

HAPPINESS.................93

PAIN.................97

CRITICISM.................101

SERENITY...................................105

SATISFACTION.........................109

LOVE..113

FRIENDSHIP..............................117

COMPARISONS..........................121

DOUBT.......................................127

REALITY.....................................131

HEALTH......................................135

SPIRIT..141

MIND..145

BODY..149

TIME...155

LIFE..161

SECURITY..................................165

CRISIS..169

RIGHTS......................................173

TABLE OF CONTENTS

THE YOU OF TOMORROW.....177

MAKING ROOM.....183

HOPE.....187

GROWTH.....191

CHANGE.....195

DESTINY.....199

CHOICE.....203

VISION.....207

PURPOSE.....211

OPTIMISM.....215

EMPOWERMENT.....219

CONFIDENCE.....223

KNOWING.....227

COMPASSION.....231

SHARING.....235

GENEROSITY.....239

DEDICATION

For my daughters, Samantha and Francesca:

 may peace be your constant companion
 as you journey through life.

INTRODUCTION

Quieting the noise in your mind. Accepting yourself and your life for what is is. Worrying less. Comparing yourself to no one. Loving yourself. Fearing nothing. To achieve this state of being is to achieve peace, a place where few reside and many seek. It's the ability to deal with the world, your life, and the people in it with calm, serenity, and confidence. Finding peace in your heart is returning to the innocence and love of the child within. It is letting go of the past, trusting yourself, and opening up your mind to the possibilities. It is surrendering yourself to live fully and lovingly in the present.

Finding peace in your heart is coming to terms with all that you've been, all that you are and all that you will be. The process is multi-dimensional and touches many aspects of your life. It takes time and patience to enter a state of true peace. There has been so much that has happened in your life—all the events of your childhood, teen years and young adult experiences that you carry with you today. Sometimes the past clouds today and prevents you from seeing tomorrow. To come to terms with yourself and your life, we first need to contemplate what *was*—our past. Then we can better deal with the present and plan for the future.

This book deals with ways to find peace of mind

through working with the three main time components of your life:

THE YOU OF YESTERDAY: This is the child within you that houses any anger and pain of youth and growing up.

THE YOU OF TODAY: This is what *is*, what you are today and how you live your life.

THE YOU OF TOMORROW: This is the hopeful, dreaming you—that part of you which looks at what *may be* and what *can be*.

Grouped in three phases of your life, you will look into aspects of the way you think, feel, and see yourself and others. With carefully crafted thoughts and suggestions contained in the following pages, you have the opportunity to reassess how you live your life, to contemplate, to forgive and to accept. We only have one time around. This is not a dress rehearsal. This is, in fact, a wonderful life, with you at its core, able to live life to its fullest.

Much of the focus of the thoughts on finding peace of mind is on *today*. While it is very important to come to terms with the past and to have a positive outlook for the future, the fact is that we wake up to *today*, to what life is now, not what it could or should be. Once you have taken the time to come to terms with your past, as best as possible, then you are ready for the real journey—that is, to find peace of mind with today, with the life that you have now at hand. Once you think about and work on how to make it

work for you *today*, then you can look forward to *tomorrow* with a sparkle in your eye and a glow in your smile.

Peace in your heart comes from a stillness, a silence in which you are at one with yourself and the world, in harmony. To begin the process, why not take some time to be still, to be quiet for about thirty minutes? Go to a relaxing place, close your eyes and be still. Do nothing and relax. You may find this hard to do and itch to get up and run an errand, make a phone call or go to the kitchen. Restrain yourself from the doer, the go-getter, the "busy bee" that consumes you all day, everyday. Now it is time to soothe your soul. To do so, you need commitment, discipline and interest.

By picking up this book, you have said that you are interested in expanding your horizons, in going beyond the complacency and routine of your life, as happy and safe as it may be. You are saying that who you are today is not enough. You may be thankful that you have your health, a good job, a loving family, yet you are not at peace. You may worry and compare yourself to others. You may wish things were somehow different and find yourself saying "If only I had this..." or "If only I was that..."

At a certain level, dissatisfaction is good when the emotion is channeled into a positive affirmation of striving to be the best you can be. However, like most of us, there is probably a little part of you that is uncomfortable and unaccepting of yourself and others.

Striving for positive

change is a challenge when you're torn inside. Finding peace in your heart releases the permission for you to have a more centered view of life. People, events, and experiences come into a fine focus and become clearer.

Often when we are speaking with people, we psychologically place a mirror in front of ourself. We filter comments by how they reflect on us, by how we feel, without taking into account that we may have nothing to do with what the other person is saying or doing. How often have you reacted to someone's comments with "I didn't do anything," or thought, "She probably thinks I'm incompetent"?

Instead, you have the opportunity to react from a base of confidence, security and love. You can think, "Can

I do anything to help?" Or just acknowledge someone's own concern or pain with, "I understand. You must feel pretty bad about it." This is one example of how finding inner peace will help you gain strength, confidence and serenity. Inner peace will allow you to look towards yourself and others with acceptance and forgiveness, with a more positive outlook and with greater love.

While reading this book, keep in mind that the best results will come to those who make a commitment to evolve. Reading, in and of itself, is not enough. It is the first part. The second part of the process to find peace of mind is doing something about it— demonstrating by your actions and behavior that you are evolving, reaching a higher plane, stretching your potential,

pushing the envelope.

Take one day at a time.
Step by step, you will journey along
the path towards peace of mind. Give
yourself the room, the time and the
love to do it now, for we only go
around once.

Here's to making the best of
life and to being the best we can be by
starting with our search for peace of
mind.

Enjoy the journey!

I. THE YOU OF YESTERDAY

Learning from our mistakes. Picking yourself up from defeat. Loving and being loved. Tears and smiles. Our experiences of joy and pain in our past contribute to who we are today. From the time of infancy, our subconscious mind has recorded the affections, emotions, pains, and joys of childhood. Perhaps as a little child you were told that you weren't good enough, or that you should be more like your brother or sister or even the neighbor's child. No doubt these comments, whether intentional or not, hurt—particularly if coming from your parents. An indelible scar is left.

Attempting in vain to please. Looking for control. Fearing abandonment. Seeking approval. All of these ways of dealing with people, with the world around us, creates a battle in our hearts and in our minds. Three of the most common ways we perpetuate a vicious cycle of inner chaos are: looking to others for validation, expecting that others will act as we desire, and trying to be something we're not.

The inner chaos results in a constant repetition of "If only...": "If only I had more money..."; "If only I were prettier, thinner, happier..." On and on it goes. There is never enough.

The roots of this dissatisfaction can be found in your past. While we cannot rewrite the past, we can change

how we deal with our inner demons, fears, and insecurities related to past experiences.

The choice is yours. The rewards can be innumerable if, on your path to finding peace of mind, you truthfully look into your past with forgiveness and confidence, knowing that you can wrap up your worries and "if onlys" in a little private gift box addressed to you alone. You can then place this imaginary gift box on a shelf in the far corner of your mind, barely visible, in no way interfering with who you are today and what you will become tomorrow.

It's time to put your past behind you.

CHILDHOOD

There are only two lasting bequests we can hope to give our children. One of these is roots; the other, wings.

—Hodding Carter

Anything can be changed. It is up to you to redirect any negative and unproductive memories of childhood to a more useful place in your life. Most of us harbor a few painful moments and feelings from our childhood, from how we were treated by our parents, teachers, siblings, family, and friends.

If you're one of the few who had an ideal childhood and think you could never be a better parent than your parents were, you deserve to be honored as probably one of the luckiest people on the planet. Most of us, while we love our parents and family, can create a nice-size list of what we would do differently if we could.

Now is the time to rid yourself of what didn't go right and what you didn't have

growing up. Take a moment to write down all the wonderful things you had when you were growing up that you are thankful for. Next to that list, write down the things that hurt you, that caused you to feel pain, fear, and distrust. On the same piece of paper, next to each of the painful things listed, write a note of forgiveness, of understanding and of the bright side of what was painful at the time. Seek to redirect the pain towards a positive, soothing thought, of the sweet, fresh lemonade that you can make out of the lemon.

Some may prefer to redirect their thoughts using their mind along with, or instead of, a pen and paper. In that case, think of a pleasant thought from childhood. Close your eyes and imagine the colors, brightness, and size of this happy image in your head. Now, think of the painful memory.

Take it and make it small, smaller, dull, duller, and less colorful than the happy memory. As the unhappy memory shrinks, put it in a tiny corner in your mind where you can't see it. It doesn't deserve a big, bright spot in your life. The positive emotion deserves center stage in all its glory.

Our experiences in childhood serve to form the adults we are today. While much of what occurred was thrust upon us, we have the responsibility today to make the best of it. This starts with forgiveness. Forgive those who hurt you and those whom you hurt. It's okay to be angry. It's not okay to carry that anger around to the point where it interferes with your happiness and peace of mind today.

Healing by learning to love the child inside is

one of the first steps to
finding peace of mind.

ACTS OF CHILDHOOD

Go to a park and play

Ride a merry-go-round

Skip

Jump

Take an afternoon nap

Look through your school picture
   albums and smile

Think about your best childhood
   friend

Remember the good times

Eat a popsicle

Go for a bike ride

Put on rollerskates

CHILDHOOD

MY ACTS OF CHILDHOOD

_____

_____

_____

_____

_____

_____

_____

_____

_____

PARENTS

To bring up a child in the way he should go, travel that way yourself once in awhile.

—Henry Wheeler Shaw

PARENTS

No other people in the world have more influence on us than our parents. Whether we like it or not, whether you are a parent yourself today or not, the truth is that there are no perfect parents. Parents do the best that they can with what they've got.

As children we look to our parents for approval, for direction, for love, for affection, and for security. Whether our families were rich or poor, small or large, functional or dysfunctional, our parents tried to show us how we should live our lives. As adults, we have the opportunity to question some of the beliefs imparted on us and resolve any leftover anger and hurt. It is up to us to rid ourselves of this excess baggage if we are to enjoy the journey of life to its fullest.

There are no universities that offer degrees in parenting. You learn it in the school of life. If we treat our children with love, kindness, and understanding, allowing them to explore and nourish their curiosity, we provide them with unlimited potential growth and enrichment.

Coming to terms with our parents is essential to coming to terms with ourselves, with our inner voice that instills the confidence and peace of mind to wake up each day and face the world with joy and purpose. You are probably more critical of yourself than your parents ever were when you think about it. Maybe your parents said hurtful things now and then. Do you find yourself thinking that you are less than competent, that you are a failure and will never make something of yourself and have the life you so desire? Let go of being so cruel to yourself. Let go of the parental voice within and listen to the positive, confident part of you. Invite the *loving you* to come out, to surrender to the beauty and potential that awaits you.

ACTS OF PARENTHOOD

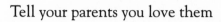

Tell your parents you love them

Say "I love you" to your kids at least once a day

Look forward, not backward

Be the best parent you can be

Treat your kids with respect

Forgive yourself for any anger or guilt you may feel

Remember, you have only one father and one mother

Make every day Mother's Day and Father's Day

PARENTS

MY ACTS OF PARENTHOOD

Mistakes

A life spent making mistakes is not only more honorable but more useful than a life spent in doing nothing.

—George Bernard Shaw

MISTAKES

Who hasn't made a few mistakes? We all have done something wrong, made a few bloopers, disappointed people important to us. From the time we were babies trying to walk, we fell down more times than we could count. Knowing that a part of being human is making mistakes, we can then begin to let go of the fear of failure and open our mind to growth, change and learning. The challenge is in not looking at the times we fell, but in sharpening our focus on how many times we've gotten back up.

Think of the three biggest mistakes you've made in the past. Relive the hurt, frustration, and embarrassment. Now take this psychic pain and forgive yourself. Forgive yourself and those you may have disappointed. It was not your intention to cause

pain to yourself or others.
By forgiving ourselves, we
transform the psychic pain into
more positive thoughts that are loving. Give yourself permission to make
a mistake now and then.

ACTS OF MISTAKES

Call a friend to say you're sorry

Forgive someone today

Figure out the things you have learned
   from the biggest mistakes you've made

Try saying "So what if I made a mistake. What's the worst that can happen?"

Find the good in imperfection, not in
   being perfect

Give yourself a break

Give others a break

Keep trying

Stretch to reach your potential

Grab a star

MISTAKES

MY ACTS OF MISTAKES

_____

_____

_____

_____

_____

_____

_____

_____

_____

_____

FORGIVENESS

Never does the human soul appear so strong as when it foregoes revenge, and dares forgive an injury.

—E. H. Chapin

FORGIVENESS

Finding peace of mind starts with forgiving yourself and the people in your past. Forgiveness means letting go of the hurt, pain, anger, and fear that is in our minds. These negative, unproductive emotions serve to cloud our lives. The sun's rays can only shine through once we have lifted the cloud. Only we can lift the cloud. No wind or outside force will erase the pain of the past. Our faith and love will dim the brightness and dull the pain of any unpleasant memories that influence us to this day. We are no longer fearful. There is nothing to fear but what we imagine. Forgiving ourselves, our parents, family, friends, old loves, and people we met along the way, serves to illuminate our imagination, to free our mind, to think positive, enriching thoughts...to make room for peace.

Forgiveness starts with yourself.

ACTS OF FORGIVENESS

Forgive yourself

Forgive those you hurt

Forgive those who hurt you

Be friends again

Look the other way

Let unimportant things slide

Talk it out

Start over again

Pick up where you left off

FORGIVENESS

MY ACTS OF FORGIVENESS

_____

_____

_____

_____

_____

_____

_____

_____

_____

_____

ACCEPTANCE

I think somehow, we learn who we really are and then live with that decision.

—Eleanor Roosevelt

The tried-and-true, equine expressions of "You can't teach an old horse new tricks" and "You can lead a horse to water, but you can't make it drink" apply a lot more to human nature than to horses. Why fight it? Why push? A calmness and clarity arise when you learn to accept what is as what is. Too often we look back on our past and wonder, "If only I had done this..." or "What if this or that never happened...?"

Now is the time to turn all these "Ifs" into "So what ifs...?" That's right. So what if I had gotten a law degree? So what if I hadn't married so young? So what if I had taken that job? So what? Thinking about your past in a "So what if...?" way allows you to toss your cares away with the wind. It doesn't change the past. What's done is done. What changes is

your view of the past. Your mind now has the opportunity to be cleansed and open to the love and joy of life today.

The road to peace of mind is fraught with landmines from the past, ready to deter you from a loving, calm and serene existence—when you least expect it! Accepting the past and recasting your negative thoughts into loving, positive lessons and experiences that were essential ingredients in making up the complete person you are today brings you one step closer to finding peace.

ACTS OF ACCEPTANCE

Love your body
Love your mind
Love your life
Love others
Love yourself

ACCEPTANCE

MY ACTS OF ACCEPTANCE

_____

_____

_____

_____

_____

_____

_____

_____

_____

_____

PURPOSE

*Life is made up of desires that seem big
and vital one minute, and little and
absurd the next. I guess we get what's
best for us in the end.*

—Alice Caldwell Rice

PURPOSE

There is a reason for all that has happened in the past. Yesterday's events and experiences form the threads of the tapestry of life. The wonderful lines on your face mark the time that has passed in which you experienced the pain and pleasure of growth, of youth, of maturity and of wisdom. Wiser are we now for we have lived.

Why are you here? What is the meaning to your life? Only you possess the answer. From deep within your mind, you can begin the search to understand all that has happened, all that is and all that will become. For there is a purpose to this madness. Having kissed some toads, you recognized your prince when he came along. Having jumped from one job to the next, you realized more and more what you wanted to do and, sometimes more

importantly, what you
didn't want to do.

There is a method to the
madness in the grand scheme of life.
Some call it a divine order. Others
call it fate. However you choose to
view it, know deep within your heart
that there is a purpose to your life and
all that has gone before you served to
bring you to where you are today. It is
up to you to recognize and embrace
your life's purpose.

Acts of Purpose

Answer the question "What do I want
to be when I grow up?" Then, do it—
no matter what your age or circum-
stance.

PURPOSE

MY ACTS OF PURPOSE

_____

_____

_____

_____

_____

_____

_____

_____

_____

_____

UNDERSTANDING

We may have all come on different ships,
but we're in the same boat now.

—Martin Luther King, Jr.

UNDERSTANDING

Part of letting go of the past is reaching a level of understanding with the people, places and events of yesterday. With compassion for yourself and for those who have touched your life, seek to understand why people treated you in a certain way and how that has affected the way you became who you are today. Through this process of understanding, we can strive to eliminate any sense of distance or sense of victimization and take responsibility for our past.

By seeking to understand our past with love and acceptance, we can then more easily understand today. There are no more powerful words than when a friend says, "I understand how you feel" and truly means it. Seek to understand others and the world around you by first understanding yourself.

Acts of Understanding

Hug a lot

Listen a lot

Care a lot

UNDERSTANDING

MY ACTS OF UNDERSTANDING

_____

_____

_____

_____

_____

_____

_____

_____

_____

_____

PRIDE

Though pride is not a virtue, it is the parent of many virtues.

—M. C. Collins

PRIDE

Our past created who we are today—
the genetics, the culture, the religion,
the ethnicity. The fabric of our
being was woven from birth. Take
pride in who you are and where you
came from. Rid yourself of doubt,
embarrassment, and fear of what
others may think. Stand tall with the
pride and knowledge that you are
unique—a beautiful mix of history, of
language, of color, and of spirit.

Taking pride in who we are is
important if we are to share our mind
and spirit with the world. Accepting
our individuality allows us to look
outward and not be so preoccupied
with what others think, for we do
not know what others think. Our
imagination tells us that. It is up to
us to redirect our images to
positive, healthy, and
righteous thoughts. Know

in your heart that you are
unique and beautiful.

ACTS OF PRIDE

Recite ten things of beauty about
 yourself

Learn about your heritage

Enjoy your uniqueness

Delight in your oneness with others

PRIDE

MY ACTS OF PRIDE

_____

_____

_____

_____

_____

_____

_____

_____

_____

_____

EMOTIONS

Some people feel with their heads and think with their hearts.

—G. C. Lichtenberg

EMOTIONS

When thinking of the past, what emotions come to mind? How much of your past is laden with thoughts of joy, pleasure, laughter, and love? Or are your thoughts more of sadness, tears, regrets, and pain? All of these emotions are natural, for our past is a mixture of the positive and the negative, the good and the bad, the happy and the sad. Now is the time to let go of negative emotions, to heal the old wounds and get on with today.

Many of us store our pain in the very back corners of our mind. Only when a crisis erupts or some serious event occurs do we bring forth our deepest pain. From this pain erupts fear—fear that things will repeat themselves, that they will be no different and perhaps worse. And well they should be, for if we continue to harbor negative, painful emotions from the past, whether consciously or subconsciously, we are blocked from realizing a state of joy in the present.

In our search for peace of mind, we must strive to deal with the emotions of our past, put them to rest, and set them free. We must free ourselves of the burden of yesterday and open ourselves to the promise of today.

ACTS OF EMOTION

Smile when you want to frown

Laugh it off

Draw a happy face

Tell someone you love them

Sing your favorite song in the shower

EMOTIONS

MY ACTS OF EMOTIONS

_____

_____

_____

_____

_____

_____

_____

_____

_____

_____

OBSTACLES

None of us can help the things life has done to us. They're done before you realize it, and once they're done they make you do other things until at last everything comes between you and what you'd like to be, and you have lost your true self forever.

—Eugene O'Neill

OBSTACLES

Along the way, you've probably had many obstacles. Perhaps divorce, illness, family relation problems, hard economic times or death have taken you on emotional roller-coaster rides. Somehow you've hurdled these obstacles. Maybe in some cases you've stepped aside and shielded yourself from the blows. Many of us lead lives of silent desperation. Now is the time to recognize the many obstacles you were up against and appreciate how you've overcome, how you've risen to the challenge.

Patting yourself on the back is a good thing. Only you know what you've been through. Only you can acknowledge and reward yourself for all that you've become. By recognizing the obstacles and acknowledging your accomplishments, you can better perceive how

you will overcome what
faces you today. Your increased
confidence will spur you on
toward realizing your dreams, being
the best you can be, and finding the
cherished inner peace you seek and
deserve.

ACTS OF OBSTACLES

Pat yourself on the back for how
  far you've come

Write each obstacle you've faced on a
  piece of paper and think how you've
  overcome each one

Throw the paper away and yell,
  "Hooray!"

See the glass as half-full

Eliminate the word "can't"

OBSTACLES

MY ACTS OF OBSTACLES

_____

_____

_____

_____

_____

_____

_____

_____

_____

_____

BAGGAGE

One of the oddest things in life, I think, is
the things one remembers.

—Agatha Christie

BAGGAGE

If we all put our emotional baggage in a suitcase, there's no doubt we could fill a plane. But where would we be headed? Nowhere and fast.

All the baggage that we bring into our lives today is inhibiting. Our goal is to recognize the baggage and let it go. Open the door to the plane in midflight and throw the suitcase out, letting it fall into a million pieces as it plummets to earth. You don't need it anymore.

The only baggage you'll carry with you today is the baggage of pleasant thoughts from the past. The rest is of no use. Only by emptying all the old suitcases and choosing not to carry around the excess baggage that weighs us down will our minds and hearts be ready to surrender to the possibilities.

We must first empty our minds of the old baggage before we can embark on the journey toward peace.

ACTS OF BAGGAGE

Buy new luggage

Throw out the old luggage

Put all of your negative thoughts in a little box and place it in the far corners of your mind where it can't be found

BAGGAGE

MY ACTS OF BAGGAGE

_____

_____

_____

_____

_____

_____

_____

_____

_____

_____

II. The You Of Today

Living today to the fullest is the surest road to peace. Nothing we can do will change the past. All the worrying and pain we carry over from yesterday only cast an impenetrable shadow over our ability to be happy today.

What we can do, however, is change the way we think about the past by placing it in its proper perspective. The real challenge is to keep our mind on what *is*, not what *was* or what *will be*. Like a fine athlete, the challenge is to focus our eyes on the ball and not think about the last play or what might happen in the next period.

Finding peace is a day-by-day process. Sometimes you'll take two steps forward and one step backward and wonder if you'll ever get there. The peace of mind you seek resides in your life today. At times, it's hard to see with all the noise, worry and fears of everyday life. The best way to help you reach into your soul, into the corners of your mind where peace of mind awaits, is to start working on it today.

If you could change one thing about yourself, what would it be? You probably have a list a mile long and find it hard to just pick one thing. Yes, we are our own worst critic. It's time now to make peace with yourself, with your body, with your fears, with your regrets and with your doubts.

Let's start today.

PERMISSION

One by one the sands are flowing,
One by one the moments fall;
Some are coming, some are going;
Do not strive to grasp them all.

—Adelaide Proctor,
"One By One"

PERMISSION

Give yourself permission to breathe.
Imagine how wonderful it feels to take
a big, deep gulp of fresh spring air. In
your life, give yourself the chance to
breathe freely and deeply.

Too often, in this rush-about
world, we are running from place to
place, from appointment to appointment, from one stoplight to the next.
Life is surely demanding. Most families
today have two incomes. So whether
you are married or single, you probably
have the demands of a job. Mount on
this the commitments that we have to
take care of others, to take care of our
house and to take care of ourselves. It's
no wonder we forget to take time for
ourselves.

Permission to breathe can
mean permission to do
nothing, to do whatever

you want, or to not do what you don't want to do. It has to do with flexibility and giving yourself a break. You make the rules and you're probably your own worst critic. Well, now is as good a time as ever to put the critic aside and give yourself an "A" for being you.

Give yourself permission to cry, to be emotional, to be lethargic, giddy, dumb, late—to be whatever it is you feel. Always jogging on the treadmill of life is tiring. Jump off and give yourself permission to do something new, different, or scary. Give yourself permission to break new ground, to explore all that is you.

PERMISSION

ACTS OF PERMISSION

Take a long, luxurious bubble bath

Keep the answering machine on

Sleep in

Get a massage, a facial, and a manicure

Take a walk in the garden

Leave the bed unmade today

Don't get out of bed today

Sit by the fireplace and dream

Throw away your "Things To Do" list

MY ACTS OF PERMISSION

_____

_____

_____

_____

_____

_____

_____

_____

PERMISSION

MY ACTS OF PERMISSION

_____

_____

_____

_____

_____

_____

_____

_____

_____

_____

ATTITUDE

Be pleasant until ten o'clock in the morning
and the rest of the day will take care of
itself.

—Elbert Hubbard

ATTITUDE

Anticipate the positive. Looking at the world through rose-colored glasses is not a bad idea these days. Things are the way they are. It is up to us to choose to view the world and ourselves in a positive or negative way. If a glass has a few ounces of juice in it, it has just that: a few ounces of juice in it. We are the ones who choose to see the glass as either half-empty or half-full. We have the same choice with our lives. If we expect that 80 percent of the time things will be O.K., with the usual little ups and downs, and at the same time expect that 10 percent of the time we'll be on top of the world and 10 percent of the time we'll feel like we've hit rock bottom, then we are better equipped to live today at 100 percent. We can live fully in the present.

The difference is in our

attitude. With an open mind that invites love and accepts ourselves and others, our fears will soon vanish. Often we find people that have poor attitudes and are afraid of something. They are afraid of being rejected, of failing, of being embarrassed, of making a mistake, and on and on. Usually, the bad attitude comes from within.

No one is telling them that they should be fearful. Sometimes it is subconscious, and they don't realize it themselves. The good news is that we have the power to change our attitude from fear to love, to embrace life and not push it away.

We all get down on ourselves from time to time. If once in a blue moon, you're depressed or so upset that you're virtually paralyzed by your worries and fears, that's part of being human.

ATTITUDE

We're perfect in God's eyes, but have a way to go in our own eyes. When you find yourself down in the proverbial dumps, try lifting your spirits by doing something new or something that will make you feel great.

Fresh air and exercise are sure ways to brighten a sulky attitude. Take a nice, long walk and leave your watch behind. Go for a bike ride. Sit on a park bench with your eyes open to the beauty around you while you enjoy the sounds of the kids playing, the dogs barking, the old-timers telling tales, and the leaves whistling in the trees. If you need an attitude adjustment and want to stay at home, why not read a great book or magazine with the phone off the hook? Or take a luxurious nap or give yourself a facial and manicure? Better yet, pamper yourself

and get a professional
facial, manicure, or massage.
Do something good for yourself
at least once a day. A bright attitude
beckons peace of mind.

ACTS OF ATTITUDE

Make lemonade out of a lemon

MY ATTITUDE ADJUSTMENTS

_____

_____

_____

_____

_____

_____

_____

_____

_____

_____

SILENCE

Learn to get in touch with silence within yourself and know that everything in this life has a purpose. There are no mistakes, no coincidences. All events are blessings given to us to learn from.

—Elizabeth Kubler-Ross

SILENCE

When was the last time you heard complete silence? The noise in our mind and the noise outside can be distracting at best, and deafening at worst. Silence is an unfamiliar state of mind for most of us. In silence, however, lies the ability to hear, to get in touch with ourselves and our potential.

Try sitting or lying in a comfortable place for thirty minutes and just doing nothing. This is not an easy task. If we are to find peace, we must first slow down, relax, be at one with ourselves. It will be easy to turn off the television, radio, telephone and close the door. The challenge is to turn off the noise in our mind...to be silent. This thirty minutes may feel like an eternity. Afterwards, you will feel rested, cleansed, and clear-eyed in the quiet of your private world.

If you can't resist doing something in your silence, try meditation, yoga, or tai chi and welcome peace into your silent retreat.

Acts of Silence

Listen—do not anticipate

Meditate

Try yoga

Enjoy the sounds of the waves crashing on the beach

Have a conversation with your soul

SILENCE

MY ACTS OF SILENCE

_____

_____

_____

_____

_____

_____

_____

_____

_____

_____

TOLERANCE

Tolerance is the positive and cordial effort to understand another's beliefs, practices, and habits without necessarily sharing or accepting them.

—Joshua Liebman

TOLERANCE

We all feel comfortable with that which is familiar. With this comfort, we generally tend to seek those people and things which are similar to us, to our beliefs and ideas. It is a grand person who accepts and respects that which is different. To tolerate is to say, "You are different from me and I from you. That's O.K." By allowing someone the ability to be themselves without criticism and judgment, we begin to tolerate.

Tolerance invites peace to gently enter your life. We clear our minds of negative thoughts and differences, and we allow love and an open mind to flourish. This is not to say that you should change your belief systems or adopt someone's behavior. Rather, tolerating others enables you to give someone the space and the permission

to be who they are. It is a
sign of respect for our fellow
man.

Allowing tolerance to enter
our lives is as soothing as a welcome
breath of fresh spring air. We stop
judging and start loving. Our fears and
thoughts of differences transform
themselves to gestures of acceptance
and recognition of all the diversity
that is life itself. We share the vision
that differences are good and healthy,
while at the same time realizing that
we do not have to share someone's
belief. Rather, we tolerate what is
unique in this everchanging world of
ours. To tolerate is to welcome inner
peace into your life.

TOLERANCE

ACTS OF TOLERANCE

Reach out to someone in need

Give your time to a charity

Give your money to a cause

Experience what's on the other side of
the tracks

Bite your tongue

Walk a mile in your brother's shoes

Count to ten

Listen—don't speak

Inquire—don't tell

Accept—don't judge

Live and let live

My Acts of Tolerance

_____

_____

_____

_____

_____

_____

_____

_____

TOLERANCE

MY ACTS OF TOLERANCE

_____

_____

_____

_____

_____

_____

_____

_____

_____

_____

THE PRESENT

Children enjoy the present because they
have neither a past nor a future.

—Jean de La Bruyère

THE PRESENT

All we have is today. The past is gone. The future is yet to be. While our body lives in the present, our mind is often caught up with reruns of yesterday's news, as we worry about the future.

What good is it to worry about your bills for instance? Worrying doesn't get them paid or reduce your potential for more bills to come. Wondering why they got so high is fruitless if we don't change our behavior today. By focusing on the present—*on today*—we redirect our thinking toward ways of earning the income to pay off the debt, of figuring out a payment schedule that works, of not buying that unnecessary item on the credit card today, and maybe of even paying cash only for anything outside of the normal, household bills.

By living life to the fullest, as if each day were our last, we open ourselves to all the beauty and simple pleasures that abound. All we have to do is take the time to smell the roses, to appreciate the color of the freshly blooming flower in our yard, to savor the smells of food we are cooking, to tell someone we love them. Living today to its fullest without cluttering our mind with past hurt and future fears is a liberating process. We free ourselves to enjoy what *is*, not what *was*, or what *could* or *should be*.

ACTS OF THE PRESENT

Stop and smell the roses

Appreciate ten things of beauty
around you

Catch yourself worrying and adjust
the volume

Don't look backwards

Live moment by moment

Live as though this were the last day
of your life

Enjoy all that you have and all that
you are

My Acts of The Present

_____

_____

_____

_____

_____

_____

_____

_____

The Present

My Acts of the Present

_____

_____

_____

_____

_____

_____

_____

_____

_____

_____

HAPPINESS

The greatest happiness you can have is knowing that you do not necessarily require happiness.

—William Saroyan

HAPPINESS

We can find happiness today if we only look. Happiness is in our hearts and asks only to be celebrated and valued. It comes from within. If we fill our mind with pleasant thoughts and try to look on the bright side, we invite happiness.

No amount of money, possessions, or ego gratification can bring us happiness. There is no such thing as the perfect car, house, job, or person to make us happy. Peace of mind comes with the recognition that happiness is the state of mind we choose. Being happy today enables us to be happy forever. Today is what counts.

Our fears try to prevent us from feeling joy and pleasure. The fearful part of us would like us to be in a constant state of watching over our shoulder and of doubting the future. Imagine going to be fitted for new glasses. Your sight will be improved. You will see things more clearly. Consider adjusting your mind in a similar way. As unproductive, unhelpful thoughts creep into your consciousness, replace them with better-fitting thoughts that focus on joy and pleasure.

ACTS OF HAPPINESS

Give of yourself to others

Do something good for yourself today and every day

Make a friend

Laugh

Smile

Sing

HAPPINESS

MY ACTS OF HAPPINESS

_____

_____

_____

_____

_____

_____

_____

_____

_____

_____

PAIN

There is no such thing as pure pleasure;
some anxiety always goes with it.

—Ovid (43 B.C.–A.D. c. 18)

PAIN

We have all been hurt in the past. Someone has disappointed us along the way. Our old lovers, friends, our family have let us down at some point. We have all been slighted at some point in our jobs where some pain resulted to our ego, if not our spirit. Pain is a part of life. Without it, we would not grow and learn.

It hurts to fall down and skin your knee. As a child, if you hadn't done it so much, you wouldn't have learned how to ride a bike, to roller-skate, and to just be a kid. Feeling some pain is necessary to feeling alive. The question is how we deal with the pain.

Many of us have a tendency to not allow a wound to heal. It takes time and forgiveness to let mental pain go its

own way. Holding grudges and harboring anger will do no good. The pain, though it may be buried, lingers.

To find peace, we must deal with our pain. Recognize it and work through the mourning process. Let go of your anger and move on. With pain in our hearts and mind, there is no room for peace to enter. Welcome peace by forgiving and moving on.

ACTS OF PAIN

Forgive...Forgive...Forgive

PAIN

MY ACTS OF PAIN

_____

_____

_____

_____

_____

_____

_____

_____

_____

_____

_____

CRITICISM

To escape criticism—do nothing, say nothing, be nothing.

—Elbert Hubbard

CRITICISM

Criticism is all around us. People get paid to critique the movies we see, the books we read, and the products we buy. Finding fault and judging are best left to the critics. In our own lives, we often tend to be our own worst critic. Have you ever exaggerated in your own mind a passing comment your boss may have made and suddenly think you're going to get fired? Do you find that when your friend comments that you look good today, you think to yourself, "That means I must not look good all the time"?

Now is the time to silence the inner critic. You are perfect. You are doing the best with what you've got, and that's okay. Once you begin to lighten up on yourself, you can open your mind to others and lift the veil of judgment.

It is exhausting to be critical all the time. Give yourself a break and leave the critiquing to the experts.

ACTS OF CRITICISM

Be constructive in your comments

Let it be

See the silver lining

Give someone the benefit of the doubt

Give yourself the benefit of the doubt

CRITICISM

MY ACTS OF CRITICISM

_____

_____

_____

_____

_____

_____

_____

_____

_____

_____

SERENITY

God give us the grace to accept with
serenity the things that cannot be
changed, courage to change the things
which should be changed, and the wisdom
to distinguish the one from the other.

—*Rienhold Niebuhr*
"The Serenity Prayer" (1934)

SERENITY

Imagine sitting on a rock perched above a still lake at sunrise. In the distance, all you can hear is the hushed shrills of the birds as the wind gently whistles through the leaves. No one is around, only you, at one with nature. Now take this picture, transpose the feeling it generates, and store it in your mind. Serenity is indeed a state of mind. It is the calm, clear way in which we live, think, and breathe.

In our desire to find serenity, some chant, pray, meditate, or practice other rituals. What we try to do is to relax our mind, still the noise, and remove the clutter in our thinking. Everyone is unique. In your quest to find peace of mind, try taking some moments out of your busy schedule to be still, to reflect, to be at one with nature and all that is the world.

Acts of Serenity

Do nothing

Allow enriching thoughts into your
life

Know in your heart that all will work
out

Help a friend

Slow down

SERENITY

MY ACTS OF SERENITY

_____

_____

_____

_____

_____

_____

_____

_____

_____

_____

SATISFACTION

Do what you can, with what you have,
where you are.

—Theodore Roosevelt

In our constant need to attain, to grow, to acquire more, to become all that we can be, we often get dissatisfied with ourselves, our lives, and those around us. On the one hand, it is O.K. to be dissatisfied when you turn this emotion into productive action. Being dissatisfied and just complaining, doing nothing about changing what you don't like is the danger. It's an easy trap to fall into.

Seeking satisfaction in all that we are allows us to become all that we can be. If we strive to accept ourselves and find pleasure in our lives, we move toward change from a base of strength. Like building a house, each brick has its role and must support one another for the house to grow and stand tall. Satisfaction with yourself enables you to build solid emotional and

psychological blocks. You are happier with today and more confident about tomorrow.

ACTS OF SATISFACTION

Give thanks to all that you are and all that you have

Appreciate life

Love yourself

Love your fellow man

Lend your time and energy to a cause greater than your own

SATISFACTION

MY ACTS OF SATISFACTION

_____

_____

_____

_____

_____

_____

_____

_____

_____

LOVE

I never loved another person the way I loved myself.

—Mae West

LOVE

Love can only enter your life if you love yourself. At the point when you can say that you know yourself, your strengths and weaknesses, the good and the bad, and you love yourself in spite of it all...this is the time for love to grow. You are its seed. As you water your soul and nourish your spirit, the love within grows. You begin to do more loving things and to share your love with others.

Love and anger do not mix well. To bring love into your life, come to terms with any anger that you are harboring. Forgive those who have hurt you. Forgive yourself for anything you might have done to fan the flames of anger. With forgiveness, love enters. Love does not judge. Love accepts. Love does not lash out. Love caresses. As you become more loving, so will love abound in your life.

ACTS OF LOVE

Hug yourself
Hug a friend
Say "Hello" to a neighbor
Lend a hand
Smile in the mirror

LOVE

MY ACTS OF LOVE

_____

_____

_____

_____

_____

_____

_____

_____

_____

_____

FRIENDSHIP

True friendship is like sound health, the value of it is seldom known until it be lost.

—Charles Caleb Colton

FRIENDSHIP

Remember the song from the sixties that went, "People...needing other people...are the luckiest people in the world"? That song has always evoked a kind of simplicity in describing our need to be needed. We are not solitary creatures. We function best in a group, with people around us who are supportive and nurturing. We don't choose our family, yet we certainly can choose our friends.

Good friends need to be cherished. It takes time to build a friendship and more time to keep one. Friends are perfect people to use as sounding boards, as shoulders to cry on, and as a safe haven from the world.

We enrich our lives with friends. By taking the time to keep up our friendships

or to make a new friend, we
are allowing love to enter our
lives. By giving, we will receive.
Be good to your friends.

ACTS OF FRIENDSHIP

Make a friend

Renew an old friendship

Call a friend

Spend time with a friend

Send your friend a card

Listen to your friend's problems—
   don't judge

Treat your family as well as you do
   your best friend

Treat yourself as well as you do your
   best friend

Make time to be with your friends

Call a friend just to say you were
   thinking of them

FRIENDSHIP

MY ACTS OF FRIENDSHIP

_____

_____

_____

_____

_____

_____

_____

_____

_____

_____

COMPARISONS

I too am a rare

Pattern

As I wander down

The garden paths

> —Amy Lowell,
> "Patterns"

COMPARISONS

Whether we like to admit it or not, we are constantly comparing ourselves to others, or to an image we have in our mind. Whether we are comparing our possessions ("Their house is nicer." "Their yard is bigger." "I wish I had a car like theirs." "Her diamond is so much bigger than mine."), or our own person ("She's got such a great figure." "Her skin is so flawless." "I wish I was as tall as her." "He has such a flat stomach."), the list goes on and on. It doesn't have to be your neighbor. Just look at the person driving next to you or the billboard in front of your face as you inch down the highway at rush hour. It all gets tiring. We can endlessly compare ourselves and come up short every time.

Essential to the process of finding peace of mind is giving up on the comparisons,

the "If only I was this or that...," or the "I should be this or that." We are our own worst enemy at times. We have to learn to let go of these comparisons.

By appreciating who we are and what we have, we can constructively, positively go forward with a focus on improving ourselves. The key is to look within. Looking outward serves only to fan the flames of envy, jealousy, and frustration.

Instead of envying others, why not appreciate the positive in others? There is enough abundance in the world for everyone. Admire and appreciate the wonderful qualities of others, and those same qualities will find their way into your life.

Peace of mind comes from within and from recognizing that all

you have to do is think about you,
about being the best that you can be,
to measure up to your own internal
yardstick built of love and acceptance.

ACTS OF COMPARISON

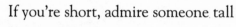

If you're short, admire someone tall

If you're brunette, admire someone
blonde

If you're poor, admire someone rich

Delight in differences

COMPARISONS

MY ACTS OF COMPARISON

_____

_____

_____

_____

_____

_____

_____

_____

_____

_____

DOUBT

There are two ways to slide easily
through life: to believe everything or to
doubt everything; both ways save us from
thinking.

—Alfred Korzybski

DOUBT

Are we ever really sure that we are doing the right thing? When we buy a car, at first it seems perfect. Then we start to think: Which color would be the best? Can we really afford it? Is there enough space? What about a smaller car, or a sportier one? Making choices in life involves some degree of doubt, of uncertainty, for we don't know what is to follow. How we live with the doubt in our lives is the question.

Once we have made a decision, we tend to rationalize it as the right thing to have done. We push aside the gnawing uncertainties and justify to ourselves that we did the right thing. We're okay—it's the other guy who needs help.

We invite peace in our lives when we put aside

the doubt, the rationaliz-
ing, the finger-pointing.
Letting go of the "what if-ing"
makes room for the surety that what
goes on before us and what we do has
a purpose. Know deep inside and
believe that your choices have
brought you experiences that served
to bring you where you are today. Your
choices filled a purpose in creating
your life and will continue to do so as
you move on the path toward peace of
mind.

ACTS OF DOUBT

Repeat "So what if...?" every time you
   find yourself doubting yourself and
   the world around you

What's the worst that can happen?

DOUBT

MY ACTS OF DOUBT

_____

_____

_____

_____

_____

_____

_____

_____

_____

_____

REALITY

It is good to have an end to journey
toward; but it is the journey that matters,
in the end.

—Ursula K. Leguin

REALITY

Accepting your life for what it *is*, and not what it *was* nor what it *could be*, is an essential step toward finding inner peace. Too often, we cloud our vision of the world and our life with thoughts that don't exist except in our mind. We think people are mad at us, don't like us, have intentionally done something bad to hurt us, and so on. This is in our own minds. The person whom you think has intentionally done you wrong may have acted out of fear for his own security, having nothing to do with you. More than likely, people's actions are based on their own fears.

By looking at reality with 20/20 vision, you will undoubtedly enrich your world. Look at your life today. Count the many blessings that you have. Focus on the little things that bring

you pleasure. Now look at yourself with clear eyes and be kind. You are your own best friend. Count the many blessings that are you.

ACTS OF REALITY

Live within your means

Count your blessings

Pinch yourself

REALITY

MY ACTS OF REALITY

_____

_____

_____

_____

_____

_____

_____

_____

_____

_____

HEALTH

Without discipline, there's no life at all.

—Katherine Hepburn

HEALTH

Feeling good, energetic, and alive is an important ingredient in finding inner peace. Good health comes from eating right, exercising, enriching your mind, and soothing your spirit. Most of us are so busy we grab a bite on the run, exercise on our way to the car and back, and are lucky if we read the paper on Sundays. Now is the time to change all that.

Develop a program that will work for you. Look at ways to eat more fruits, vegetables, and low-fat foods. Do away with the sugars, fats, and fast-food solutions. Make time to exercise...to go to the gym...to walk the stairs instead of taking the elevator...to park in the spot furthest from the entrance and walk a little farther...buy that exercise tape and get up an hour earlier to do it. Go to the library or the bookstore and get a few mind-enriching books that interest you...go to that

lecture you've always been curious about...get that audio tape about positive attitude and any other subject of interest...start that hobby you've always been interested in. Make your dreams a reality.

By being in good health, we are more easily able to turn our attention to other things that will enrich our lives. Cherish your health.

HEALTH

ACTS OF HEALTH

Eat smart

Do exercise you find fun

Get a massage

Walk

Drink lots of water

Think positive, affirming thoughts

Get a good night's sleep

Sing

Dance

Meditate

Go to a spa

Go on a diet...and stick to it this time!

Change your lifestyle for the better

My Acts of Health

HEALTH

MY ACTS OF HEALTH

_____

_____

_____

_____

_____

_____

_____

_____

_____

_____

SPIRIT

We all live with the objective of being happy. Our lives are different and yet the same.

—Anne Frank

All that is you goes beyond the matter, beyond that which we can see. Your love of life, your outlook, your vivaciousness are all parts of your spirit. When we have a brighter outlook, we see the glass a half-full, not half-empty. Enjoyment is more abundant.

Nourishing your spirit takes discipline. It's all too easy to get down on ourselves and those around us. Our ego is constantly trying to inch its way into every waking moment. We must elevate our spirit with the little things we do each day. Wear a smile instead of a frown. Laugh a bit more. Sing out loud. Compliment yourself. Compliment others. Say "I love you" to someone every day. With each lift of your spirit, you become more open to positive, enriching things, allowing them to enter your life. Peace of mind awaits.

ACTS OF SPIRIT

Smile...Laugh...Sing

Treat others with kindness

Treat yourself with kindness

Believe in something bigger than
what we know in the material world

MY ACTS OF SPIRIT

_____

_____

_____

_____

_____

_____

_____

_____

_____

_____

MIND

The brain is as strong as its weakest
think.

—Eleanor Doan

MIND

How powerful our minds are. We have the ability to influence our health, our happiness, and our dreams with our thoughts. Many patterns and habits have built up through the years to bring us to where we are today, to how we think and how we treat others. It's impossible to change the past. We can only change how we think about it.

The same is true with today. We empower ourselves through the recognition that we can positively cause change and influence our lives and the lives of others by how we think. In our seemingly constant need to be in control, we can rest easy that our mind has the power to effect change.

Enrich your mind with positive, life-affirming thoughts. Learn new ways

of thinking through reading, listening to tapes, going to lectures, and participating in groups that interest you. Experience new things. Go to someplace new for a short vacation. Take a nature walk and marvel in the beauty that abounds. Think peaceful, affirming thoughts and know in your heart that you are on the road to peace.

ACTS OF THE MIND

Do something you've always wanted to do, but were afraid to try

Learn about other ways to view life and the world

Read a lot

Ask questions

Stay curious

MY ACTS OF THE MIND

_____

_____

_____

_____

_____

_____

_____

_____

_____

_____

BODY

Then give to the world the best you have,

And the best

Will come to you.

—Madeline Bridges,
"Life's Mirror"

Be good to your body. Little aches, pains, allergies, and the stresses of everyday life cause wear and tear on our bodies. Our backs, feet, and shoulders bear the brunt of the stress. Feeling stress and tension is distracting. It takes us away, however, subconsciously, from being relaxed and fully concentrating on the things that are important.

Treat yourself to a massage and allow your tired muscles to be soothed, rubbed, and kneaded into submission. Take a bubble bath by candlelight with a glass of wine and relax. Think about exercising a bit. Taking a brisk walk is great and can be done almost anywhere. In the privacy of your home, exercise videos are great time-savers. You don't have to run to and from the gym and exercise your foot on

the gas pedal if you work
out at home.

Another important area to
enrich your body is through your diet.
Eating nutritionally sound, balanced
meals adds energy and vitality to your
days, and helps rid you of any excess
poundage that has crept up on you
over the years. Drink more water and
less caffeine. Toss the sugary and fatty
foods. Treat your body as you would
your own baby, feeding it only good,
wholesome food.

With a healthier, fitter, more
relaxed *you*, your body comes in tune
with your mind and your spirit, in your
quest to be at one in a perpetual state of
peace.

ACTS OF THE BODY

Nurture your body

Sleep

Eat well

Exercise

Think positively

Be active

My Acts of the Body

_____

_____

_____

_____

_____

_____

_____

_____

BODY

MY ACTS OF THE BODY

_____

_____

_____

_____

_____

_____

_____

_____

_____

_____

TIME

*But somehow one never had time to stop
and savor the taste of life as the stream of
it flowed by. It would be good to find
some quiet inlet where the waters were
still enough for reflection, where one
might sense the joy of the moment, rather
than plan breathlessly for a dozen
mingled treats in the future.*

—Kathleen Norris,
"Bread Into Roses"

TIME

There never seems to be enough of it—with car phones, fax machines, shopping without ever leaving your home, and hourly calendars where you even have to make an appointment to see your spouse. We are in a time-pinch. Rushing about and being busy can get crazy. Even if you have gotten fifty things off your list today, how relaxed do you really feel? There's surely another fifty things to do tomorrow.

This seemingly constant state of chaos inhibits finding peace. Sure we can say that we are busy and maybe have accomplished a lot in one day, but can we say that we feel good about it all? Are we calm or is our blood pressure elevated and our head aching more than we'd like? It's time to take control, to get a grip.

Start by making time for yourself. By saying "no" and giving yourself the permission to do only what you want to do, what is comfortable, you push off the outside pressures and demands. So what if something takes two days instead of one, or if you do it next week instead of today? Or what if you don't do it at all? What's the worst that can happen? Make time work for you. Take the time to be good to yourself.

TIME

ACTS OF TIME

Manage the expectations of others

Learn to say "no" to others and "yes"
  to yourself

Limit interruptions

Help your family to help themselves

Schedule personal time

When someone else can do it, delegate

Say "yes" to simplicity

Stop *"should-ing"*

Work backwards, plan ahead

My Acts of Time

_____

_____

_____

_____

_____

_____

_____

_____

_____

MY ACTS OF TIME

_____

_____

_____

_____

_____

_____

_____

_____

_____

_____

LIFE

Do every act of your life as if it were your last.

—Marcus Aurelius

LIFE

If you only had six months to live, how would you live your life? Now, how close are you today to where you would be if you lived like every minute counted? The gap between the two is what needs to be filled in. We only go around once. To make the most of the precious gift of life, we need to live with gusto, passion, and purpose. Take a moment to reflect on your life. What is good about it? What would you like to change? How can you do it?

Living life to its fullest will enable you to ride through the rough times, take them in stride and have the confidence to know that the good times are around the bend. Ups and downs are a part of it. We can fight it or ride with it. Coming to terms with your life, its purpose

and direction, can only
bring you closer to your
dreams.

ACTS OF LIFE

Savor each moment

Appreciate the beauty around you

Show your family that you love them

Give to someone in need

Inject passion into every day

LIFE

MY ACTS OF LIFE

_____

_____

_____

_____

_____

_____

_____

_____

_____

_____

SECURITY

I think knowing what you cannot do is more important than knowing what you can do. In fact, that's good taste.

—Lucille Ball

SECURITY

As a child, security was knowing that things familiar to us were around: our parents, our toys, our friends, our home. As adults, we seek the same security, albeit in a different form, but not much different. Our parents are replaced by our spouses. Our toys are replaced by our cars, clothes, and jewelry. Our friends are replaced more by our jobs. Our house is replaced by our bank account. The security we seek is predominantly emotional, financial, and physical.

There is a security that comes with peace of mind that does not reside on the material level. It is the inner knowing and confidence that you are safe and that things will work out for the best—that your dreams will come true. The power of positive thought will guide you.

ACTS OF SECURITY

Learn that you can take care of
  yourself

Trust yourself

Have faith

Visualize your dreams becoming reality

Know that they will be done

SECURITY

MY ACTS OF SECURITY

_____

_____

_____

_____

_____

_____

_____

_____

_____

_____

CRISIS

You must learn to be still in the midst of activity and to be vibrantly alive in repose.

—Indira Gandhi

CRISIS

We open ourselves to finding peace when we recognize that most of the time, say 80% of it, things are good, fine, O.K. Another 10% of the time, life is terrific. You feel like you can walk on air. The rest of the time, the other 10%, life seems horrible—one crisis after another. You want to scream or run and hide depending on the day. You see, crisis is a normal part of life. Without it, we wouldn't appreciate the good times and the great times.

We grow in times of crisis. We are forced to stretch, to test our limits of patience and understanding. With crisis comes change. No one generally likes too much change, and if it comes in the form of bad news, then worse yet. Change is a part of life. Just when you think the clouds will never leave, the rain-

bow appears and it's another sunny day. In times of crisis, navigate through the storm, knowing that the rainbow will appear. You just have to make it out in one piece.

Crisis is inevitable. Seeing its predictability is our choice.

ACTS OF CRISIS

Ride out the storm

Find the eye of the storm

Keep your head

Know that this too shall pass

CRISIS

MY ACTS OF CRISIS

_____

_____

_____

_____

_____

_____

_____

_____

_____

_____

RIGHTS

Let me tell thee, time is a very precious gift of God; so precious that He only gives it to us moment by moment. He would not have us waste it.

—Amelia Barr

It is within our power to have the right to choose, to say "no," to give permission. We don't always have to please, or worry about being liked. We have the right to set boundaries. Others need to know how far they can go. In fact, sometimes we need to set the limits just for ourselves.

Often we are our own worst abusers. We try to do too much and don't know how to say "no." Set up your own bill of rights, like our founding fathers did. Let it be the basis of your constitution.

ACTS OF RIGHTS

Set limits

Say "no" when you want to

Say "yes" to yourself

Rights

My Acts of Rights

_____

_____

_____

_____

_____

_____

_____

_____

_____

_____

III. THE YOU OF TOMORROW

As a child, dreaming about the way life will be, we imagined that we would grow up to be in some profession. We would have a pretty house, a family of our own and lots of animals. We spend the better half of our lives trying to build our lives to reach our dreams. In our quest, there is little time to sit still and appreciate all that we have now. We're often in such a rush to get to another place that we forget how nice the place where we are now is. It's a fine balance to strive for, in that we need to dream, to hope. Yet, we must stand grounded in the reality that is before us and appreciate the many blessings that we have. With our feet on the ground and our hands reaching for the stars, the possibilities are endless.

Looking into the future can be so seductive. We escape into a world that we create, where we have what we want, we live how we want and are happy. Dreaming is good. It's necessary.

Without hope, why live? We need hope and purpose in our lives to see a reason to live. I once saw a video that showed why certain victims of the concentration camps survived. The survivors shared a bond of hope and purpose. One wanted to finish his research in a developmental area in medical science. Another found his purpose in reuniting with his girlfriend who

had gone to the United States a year earlier. They had planned to start a family. Another survivor wanted to complete a book she was writing. They all had a reason to live, something bigger than themselves—a purpose. They were able to keep hope alive.

It is up to us to think about the future in a constructive, hopeful and purposeful way in order to realize our dreams. This is easier said than done. Too often our fears get the better of us, like the times when that piece of rich chocolate cake calls our name and we succumb, blowing any semblance of a diet we might have been on.

Fear is like the lurking predator. Persistent, it keeps knocking on our door, hoping we will succumb to its insidious lust. Fighting our fears is tough. We have to work on taming one dragon at a time, or it becomes too overwhelming.

Recognizing our fears is the surest step toward releasing them. For if we do not know they are there, then how do we figure out why we are stumbling and going in circles so much, repeating the same patterns?

Tomorrow offers all the possibilities we can imagine. You can do anything. You just have to believe it. It is a mindset. Many of the most successful people were rejected by almost everyone, before they got their break, their "chance to shine." These people believed in themselves, shook off the closed doors and rejection, picked themselves up and went on to the next opportunity. The common thread is their belief in themselves. Believing in yourself creates

unlimited possibilities.

In your quest for peace,
gently move down life's path knowing
that you *can* and *will* find it. Reach
out to your dreams, build your hopes
on a boundless tomorrow where you
will live in harmony with your past,
your present, and the many beautiful
days that await.

MAKING ROOM

Let us not go over the old ground, let us rather prepare for what is to come.

—Marcus Tullius Cicero (106–43 B.C.)

Making Room

Just as though it were springtime, unclutter your life. Out with the old and in with the new. It doesn't matter what time of year it may be. With snow on the ground or rain in the sky, there is no better season than the present to make room for peace.

Peace resides in a room with a view in the warm, quiet corner of your mind. The view is of a brilliant and sunny tomorrow. A place where few reside and many seek. Peace demands its own space in a place that only you can construct.

ACTS OF MAKING ROOM

Set aside time to think and plan

Make achieving peace of mind a
  wondrous journey, not an end
  in itself

Enjoy the journey

MAKING ROOM

MY ACTS OF MAKING ROOM

_____

_____

_____

_____

_____

_____

_____

_____

_____

_____

HOPE

There is no medicine like hope, no incentive so great, and no tonic so powerful as expectation of something tomorrow.

—O. S. Marden

HOPE

Hope is the nourishment that sustains our soul. Looking toward tomorrow with the confidence that everything you so deeply desire will happen, you are then able to go forward with confidence in all that you do and in all that you are.

ACTS OF HOPE

Say "I will" instead of "Maybe"

Visualize the outcome—in vivid shapes, colors, and sizes

Have faith in yourself

Trust

HOPE

MY ACTS OF HOPE

_____

_____

_____

_____

_____

_____

_____

_____

_____

_____

GROWTH

Growth is the only evidence of life.

—John Henry, Cardinal Newman

GROWTH

One thing is certain. Nothing stays the same. Know in your heart that whatever troubles appear overwhelming, they too shall pass. No one can predict tomorrow. Things can either happen to us, or we can make them happen.

Acts of Growth

Take responsibility

Evolve

Try a new attitude

Do something different

Do what you fear...and enjoy your
  success

GROWTH

MY ACTS OF GROWTH

_____

_____

_____

_____

_____

_____

_____

_____

_____

_____

CHANGE

The only sense that is common in the long run is the sense of change—and we all instinctively avoid it.

—*Anonymous*

CHANGE

Nothing stays the same. Would you ever have imagined your life as it is today? For all your plans and dreams, things turned out differently. You are different than you were yesterday. The sum of life's experiences takes its toll. Our challenge is to learn from our experiences, to evolve and to grow. Staying the same is boring, static. Life is for the living.

Acts of Change

Be a chameleon
Try something different
React unexpectedly
Wear a new hat

CHANGE

MY ACTS OF CHANGE

_____

_____

_____

_____

_____

_____

_____

_____

_____

_____

DESTINY

Destiny is not a matter of chance, it is a matter of choice. It is not a thing to be waited for, it is a thing to be achieved.

—William Jennings Bryan

DESTINY

Some things in life are inevitable, out of our control. That can be an intimidating thought to many. Most of us feel safe when we are in control. To be out of control, in the sense that we surrender to our destiny while making the wisest choices available, is a step toward finding peace of mind.

ACTS OF DESTINY

Surrender

DESTINY

MY ACTS OF DESTINY

_____

_____

_____

_____

_____

_____

_____

_____

_____

_____

CHOICE

A little kingdom I possess,
  Where thought and feelings dwell;
And very hard the task I find
  Of governing it well.

—Louisa May Alcott,
    "My Kingdom"

CHOICE

We can live our life with excuses and rationalizations for all that we don't have and all that we can't become, or we can choose to make something different. The choice is ours to step up to the plate and take responsibility for our actions, our situation, and our state of mind. Choose peace of mind and you are one step closer to realizing your dreams.

ACTS OF CHOICE

Take responsibility

Make choices

Make it happen

Throw away excuses

Point your finger at no one

CHOICE

MY ACTS OF CHOICE

_____

_____

_____

_____

_____

_____

_____

_____

_____

_____

VISION

Yet it is in our idleness, in our dreams, that
the submerged truth sometimes comes to the
top.

—Virginia Woolf,
"A Room of One's Own"

VISION

Seeing is believing. Opening your mind to the possibilities—to what can be and to what you want—is a state of mind. We see what we want to see. Our future is as bright as the light we shine on it.

ACTS OF VISION

Reaffirm your confidence in
  tomorrow

Draw a detailed picture of how you
  want your life to look, feel, smell,
  and be

VISION

MY ACTS OF VISION

_____

_____

_____

_____

_____

_____

_____

_____

_____

_____

_____

PURPOSE

I am the master of my fate;
I am the captain of my soul.

—William E. Henley

PURPOSE

There is a reason why you are in this world. Ask yourself, "What is the purpose to my life? What is my reason for living?" Once you have found your answer, live your life to fulfill your purpose, and peace of mind will be your constant companion.

ACTS OF PURPOSE

Find a meaning in all that you do

PURPOSE

MY ACTS OF PURPOSE

_____

_____

_____

_____

_____

_____

_____

_____

_____

_____

OPTIMISM

Ah, but a man's reach should exceed his grasp—or what's a heaven for?

—Robert Browning

OPTIMISM

Wear a smile in your heart.

ACTS OF OPTIMISM

Smile

OPTIMISM

MY ACTS OF OPTIMISM

_____

_____

_____

_____

_____

_____

_____

_____

_____

_____

EMPOWERMENT

You must do the things you think you
  cannot do.

—Eleanor Roosevelt

EMPOWERMENT

We live in a power-oriented society. Everyone is trying to be in charge and show they're in control. We often look at this as though it is outside of our control and that things are being done to us. There is magic in believing that we have the power within to be what we want, achieve what we want, and do what we want. Test the limits of your being and do what you think you cannot do.

Empowerment is taking control of your destiny, being responsible and accountable for your actions. Discard the thought that you are a victim, a pawn on life's chessboard. You have the power to see the future as you would have it and to make it come to life.

ACTS OF EMPOWERMENT

Take responsibility

Choose your own destiny

Be accountable

Don't blame

Become victimless

EMPOWERMENT

MY ACTS OF EMPOWERMENT

_____

_____

_____

_____

_____

_____

_____

_____

_____

_____

CONFIDENCE

The hopeful man sees success where others see failure, sunshine where others see shadows and storm.

—O. S. Marden

CONFIDENCE

Depending on your perspective, life can appear in a variety of colors, shades, sizes, and shapes. When you change the perspective with which you are viewing an object, doesn't the object appear to change? Confidence, as beauty, is in the eye of the beholder. No one can instill it in you. You must choose to possess it.

Your future is as bright as you make it. It hasn't happened and any images in your mind are yours and yours alone. Why not choose to take charge of your future with the confidence and surety that it will turn out just fine and that all your dreams will come true? No one has the power to tell you otherwise. Seeing is believing—and seeing with confidence is the surest step towards actualizing your dreams and realizing your goals.

ACTS OF CONFIDENCE

Think: "I can. I will."
Step with certainty
Keep your eye on the ball

CONFIDENCE

MY ACTS OF CONFIDENCE

_____

_____

_____

_____

_____

_____

_____

_____

_____

_____

KNOWING

Where there is the tree of knowledge,
there is always paradise; so say the most
ancient and the most modern serpents.

—Friedrich Nietzche

KNOWING

Live your life knowing that peace of mind is a process, a blessed journey which only the wise choose to wander.

ACTS OF KNOWING

Expand your horizons

Gain new perspectives

Enjoy the journey

Learn...learn...learn

KNOWING

MY ACTS OF KNOWING

_____

_____

_____

_____

_____

_____

_____

_____

_____

_____

COMPASSION

Fear grows out of the things we think; it lives in our minds. Compassion grows out of the things we are, and lives in our hearts.

—Barbara Garrison,
"Random Acts of Kindness"

COMPASSION

Understanding with your heart and giving of your time and emotions are the greatest acts of compassion one can bestow on a fellow human being. Our ability to be human—to feel for someone in need and to do something about it—is a great gift. Compassion is a gift you can give yourself.

ACTS OF COMPASSION

Giving—

time...heart...material possessions...love

—to those in need

COMPASSION

MY ACTS OF COMPASSION

_____

_____

_____

_____

_____

_____

_____

_____

_____

_____

SHARING

Man should not consider his material possessions his own, but common to all, so as to share them without hesitation when others are in need.

—St. Thomas Aquinas

Reaching out to others in need will result in abundance. When we find that we are caught up in our own problems and fears, the best recourse we have is to distract our self-pity by reaching out to someone. It becomes a way of life. Once accustomed to it, you will find yourself addicted to giving, to touching another's life with your time, spirit, possessions, and love. The favor will be returned tenfold.

ACTS OF SHARING

Reach out to someone

SHARING

MY ACTS OF SHARING

_____

_____

_____

_____

_____

_____

_____

_____

_____

_____

GENEROSITY

T'was her thinking of others that made you think of her.

—Elizabeth Browning

GENEROSITY

Generosity of spirit is the greatest gift you can give yourself. By giving to others, you enrich your soul and invite a warm, loving companion to be at your side as you turn the pages of your book of life. Peace of mind will gently take its place by your side. This faithful and all-knowing companion will quietly see you through.

Acts of Generosity

Give what you have

Give what you want

Give what you lack

Give of your time

Lend a hand

Lend an ear

GENEROSITY

MY ACTS OF GENEROSITY

_____

_____

_____

_____

_____

_____

_____

_____

_____

_____

About the Author

Paula Peisner Coxe was born in Los Angeles. She was educated at the University of California, Los Angeles and completed a Master's Degree in Business Administration at the University of Southern California. Ms. Coxe is a management consultant and the author of *Finding Time: Breathing Space for Women Who Do Too Much*. Paula lives and writes in Oregon with her husband and two daughters.

Don't Miss These Great Books by Paula Peisner Coxe

Finding Time: Breathing Space for Women Who Do Too Much
Learn to successfully manage time and outside demands to find the time to enjoy life more. For every woman too tired, too busy, or just too stressed to think of herself, this bestselling book shows you how to find or make time for yourself.
256 pages, ISBN: 0-942061-33-0 (paperback) $7.95

Breathing Space: A Finding Time Journal For Women Who Do Too Much
Let this elegant journal be the place where you find the peaceful time you deserve. This personal memoir designed to breathe space into the lives of busy women across the country. Filled with quotes, inspirational suggestions, and tips from *Finding Time*, *Breathing Space* reminds you that time to yourself is important. Celebrate it within the serene pages of this beautiful journal.
160 pages, ISBN: 1-57071-036-8 (paperback) $7.95
March 1995

Finding Love: Embracing The Essence Of Life
Paula Peisner Coxe has shown thousands of people the secrets to *Finding Time* and *Finding Peace*. Now she shows us how to find our greatest friend, and yet most elusive companion—love. Paula's warmth and wonderful, positive style carry *Finding Love* beyond the obvious. Let her help you solve the splendid mystery of love.
256 pages, ISBN: 1-57071-031-7 (paperback) $7.95
April 1995

To order these books or any other of our many publications, please contact your local bookseller or call Sourcebooks. Get a copy of our catalog by writing or faxing:

Sourcebooks Inc.
P. O. Box 372
Naperville, IL 60566
(708) 961-3900
FAX: (708) 961-2168
Thank you for your interest!

Also Available Are These Fine Business-Related Books From Sourcebooks—